BACK AGAINST

How The First 21 Years of My Life Has Been And

How You Can Learn Through My Experiences

Ursino Obamudi

PRAISE FOR BACK AGAINST THE WALL

"This book consists of an informative aspect as well as successfully engages the reader. It is packed with Ursino's real-life experiences in the form of a story, in combination with life lessons that can be taken away from it. This book is definitely a meaningful and enjoyable read that will leave readers engaged and enlightened."

JULIANA MILL, Harvard Graduate

"This book is amazing because it opens the reader up to Ursino's world and allows you to know the author almost on a personal level while learning valuable lessons that are proven to be useful in life. I recommend this book to people of all ages who have an earnest desire to learn, thrive and grow."

LEAH BALOGUN, Blog Writer and Podcaster

"A transparent dive into the life of Ursino whereby heartfelt vulnerable moments are shared, with lots of lessons to take from it. A book straight from the heart."

FEMI OPEDO, Aspiring Actor and YouTuber

"Ursino takes you on a journey down memory lane, and shares with you his acquired wisdom from the lessons he has learnt from a multitude of experiences in a retrospective manner. Highly and happily recommended read."

REUBEN CHUMPUKA, Aspiring Solicitor

"The beauty of BATW lies in how the author roped in his readers with the most enthralling and relatable stories and while they smile, laugh, and shake their heads in understanding, he managed to churn out several valuable life lessons. Now, Ursino has us looking for diamonds in the rough and I love it! Well done."

THEOLA MONDAY, Screenwriter

"Ursino shares aspects of his life story in which he learnt meaningful life lessons that he happily shares with us. It is a very inspirational book in gaining a sense of hope for trials & tribulations that one might encounter in life. Ursino engages with the reader creating a sense of familiarity which is something I believe makes a great book! Very proud."

VICTORIA AMUNIKORO, Student

Thanks

Table of Contents

Preface

R ight from when I was a child, I've always written short
stories but I never finished them. Because I was creative,
I tried to write a few fantasy books but I didn't see it through
because I was focused on other things. Now I am going to
write about my life so far because I am confident that my
story will impact your life. From the moment I was born in
Nigeria, my life has been full of ups and downs. I faced
terrible challenges when I was younger and as I get older, the
challenges keep increasing and it doesn't seem like it's
stopping soon. As a child, I had to overcome many obstacles
and traumatic events but that never stopped me from looking
forward and having faith in a brighter tomorrow.

As the saying goes, 'What doesn't kill you makes you
stronger.' Now, I can't complain about what I've been
through because every situation I'm in right now are due to
my past decisions. Neither my family nor the two people who
usually know most of my moves know what I'm about to
write in this book. Those two are Femi Opedo and Ayomide
Adeyanju. I bet they're reading this now, and they're happy I
mentioned their names. As you continue to read, you will get

to meet more people from my friendship group.

I am not writing this book to place myself on a pedestal to the detriment of others. I just want you to learn from my experiences and please, don't feel sorry for me too. I understand we all experience challenges regularly. But I know my story is going to touch you and give you hope during hard times. I want you to pick up this book in your good and bad moments and read through it again. I hope it encourages you to keep going and never stop.

I wrote this book because I love helping people and inspiring them too. My life's story will help you realise that no situation is permanent and change (whether good or bad) will forever remain constant. Life is as hard as you make it to be, and your life experiences shapes you into the beast you're today—no matter what situation you find yourself in. Never give up because there is always light at the end of the tunnel. You have to keep going and never stop if you want to see the light.

Some of you reading this right now might say it's too early for Ursino Obamudi, also known as sinobills, to write a book. However, there is no perfect time for anything in life. If you wait for the ideal time, you'll be waiting for the rest of your life. A feeling sparked in me recently about my aspirations. I realised that whenever anyone asked me about them, I never had a befitting answer. But, for the past eight months, I've been reading a lot of books. I realised that I enjoy reading, I love writing, and I love helping people too. So I decided I was going to become an Author; well, I will be one once this book is published.

As I write this, I'm merely 21 years old but sometimes it feels like I've lived for 100+ years. This book explains why. Every chapter in this book tells a unique story leading up to where I am today. I wouldn't be writing this book without the help of my family and friends. I want to thank all of you for never giving up on me and pushing me to where I am today. Some of you might not notice this but watching all of you grow through life doing your own thing, no matter how big or small it is has inspired me to be a better person and grind every day. You're all blessings from God in my life. Without you all, I don't think I would even be alive to tell this story.

I want to thank my parents because I literally would not exist and neither would this story without their amazing influence. God blessed my siblings and me with the most amazing parents and I honestly can't wait to repay them for all the sacrifices they have made and continue to make for their children. In due time, everyone will see me at the top, and I will finally be able to give them the life they deserve.

What you're about to read is what I feel comfortable sharing with the world. I still value my privacy but within the following eight chapters, I'll tell you the most important events that shaped my life till this present day. I'm a very straightforward person and I hate to beat around the bush, so I would only explain my experiences briefly while focusing on the important lessons. After every chapter (asides chapter 1), there will be a life lesson and even mini-life lessons in some chapters. I hope they're helpful to you and if they are, please let me know.

Although I wrote some parts of this book from an entrepreneur's perspective, it'll benefit you even if you aren't one. You have to be open-minded to fully grasp everything you are about to read too. There are also a lot of time skips to ensure the meat of the story is told properly. I barely used dates since I don't remember them correctly but I did specify the months and years so you don't feel confused while reading.

This book is filled with summaries of my most important life experiences and they are full of exciting twists. I hope you enjoy it.

Be Inspired.

Keep Going.

Never Stop.

Ursino Obamudi

Chapter 1

The Rise (My Birth), *1999*

I'm not too familiar with the story of my birth, but my mother told me I was born at noon in Nassarawa Hospital, Kano, a northern part of Nigeria. According to her, birthing me was a real challenge because even moments after giving birth to me, she wasn't allowed to leave the theatre. Before that, she had been in labour for a few days and had gone to see a friend of hers who was a doctor. The doctor told her it was nothing serious and she shouldn't worry. Amid all this, she had to be at an office event the night before my birth. She went to see Doctor Lola but didn't tell her anything about the situation because she was the paediatrician. My mother was only advised to consult a gynaecologist. Immediately my mother arrived at the hospital, her water broke. The doctor advised her to drink a castor oil concoction that was supposed to help stabilize her. The morning after, my father took my mother to the hospital with my grandmother; and I was born before midday.

After she had me, she couldn't leave the labour room

because she was losing a lot of blood. The doctor then asked her if her previous scans ever showed her that she was carrying twins. My mother responded that she had no idea, even as she continued to bleed profusely. When my mother was to be cleaned up, a petite nurse with tiny hands put her hands inside my mother and gathered enough blood to fill several big bowls. The blood was thrown out while she continued to lie on the hospital bed.

Moments later, Doctor Vasha, my mother's doctor, came to check my mother and told her she could not go home that night because she needed to have an evacuation immediately. They took her to the recovery room where she stayed with me. At one point, she needed to go to the bathroom, but when she got there, she fainted. But thankfully, someone else was there. After raising alarm, some nurses came with the doctors and they performed the evacuation successfully. My mother stayed overnight at the hospital until she went home in the early hours of the morning.

Every time she tells me the story of my birth, it assures me that I can face any situation I find myself in with faith. From this story alone, I realised that, regardless of my present status, I'm going to be a great man and I will use my talents to impact this world.

In this book, I will explain the most important parts of my life. Although it will be tough to recall the first ten years of my life with the utmost accuracy, I'll try my best.

Chapter 2

Getting Comfortable In The Gaza, *2000-2008*

I grew up in a family of seven which included my mum and dad and four siblings – three brothers and one sister. I am the fourth child. I would consider my family a close one but growing up, I wondered why my parents named me Ursino. I asked my mother what my name meant severally and she always told me that 'Ursino' is the Latin term for a grizzly bear. Honestly, I think I'm the only person you'll ever know that bears this name and this uniqueness is why I love my name so much. Also, my middle name, Osigbemhe, means 'God is with me,' and I'm the living proof that he has been.

When I was younger, my first love was football and I was gifted my first football when I was just two years old. I remember how watching football at my cousin's or my Grandmother's house together was always a lovely experience because we all supported different teams. That's where I got my competitiveness from. I hated losing back then, and it would often anger me. Once I lost, I would cry and sit in the corridor. If I wasn't watching or playing football, then I'd be going to school. I attended Spring Gate Nursery and Goldstar Primary School before I came to the UK and it was not far from my home. One of my many experiences worthy of note is how much trouble I got into because of my weak bowel. Till I clocked five, my bowels behaved exactly as they wished and it caused some issues for my classmates because whenever it happened, the class had to stop.

Living in Nigeria sometimes meant running around naked every day, especially when you're young with zero priorities and zero troubles. My parents were neither rich nor poor, but they made sure their children never lacked anything, and I'll always value them because of that. Whenever I ran around, I would always end up injuring myself. I even broke a few bones. First, my elbow split into two when I attempted to do a backflip off a bed outside. I also broke my toe when I kicked it into the ground. Now, breaking my bones wasn't even the problem. The problem was that whenever I broke any bone, my mother would first take me to a woman. This woman would apply pressure on the area so it heals better over time, and the pain that pressure causes is one of the worst feelings I've ever experienced. The only highlight in being treated by that woman was that I got to eat at my grandma's shop. And my grandmother's food was finger-licking good. It remains one of the best I've ever tasted. On some days, I daydream about having it again. But I haven't seen my grandma in thirteen years, and I miss her every day because my mother reminds me so much of her.

I don't remember much about Nigeria because I was so young. However, I experienced life-changing moments, like the time I almost died. It was a fine afternoon after a long day of school, which consisted of me playing in the playground and not understanding what was going on during my classes. My older cousins came around to pick my brother and I from primary school. I finished my final class earlier than my brother, so I had to wait for him outside with my cousins. About 10 minutes later, he came outside his classroom and held my older cousin's hand. We all started to walk home and noticed that there was more traffic than usual. We kept walking and soon, it was time for us to cross the road. Usually, we would wait until all the cars go by before crossing to the other side of the road, but it seemed like my cousins were in a rush on this day, so they crossed the road without me. At this time, I was five or six years old, so I was tiny. I couldn't wait for them to come back and get me so I decided to cross myself. I was slowly moving past vehicles until I got to the middle and narrowly made it past a car. But out of nowhere, a motorcycle came towards me at full speed and ran over me. Then I blacked out, and six hours later, I woke up in a hospital with scabs all over my entire body. According to my mother, it took a while before I could walk normally again.

When I woke up from my concussion, I went home and spent time with my family. After surviving this, nothing changed. I was still living life as usual without realising how serious the accident was. Now that I'm older, I find myself reflecting on that specific moment and every time I do that, I conclude that life is so crazy and very fragile. Anything can happen, so remaining grateful for life is so important.

A couple of months went by and it was getting closer to my birthday. Little did I know that it wouldn't be the celebration I imagined it would be. Events surrounding my sixth and seventh birthday has so far caused me to have an indifferent attitude towards birthdays. On those days, my house got robbed twice on my birthday. It wasn't a burglar case but an armed robbery. If I had not been home with my father that day, I would have either been kidnapped or injured. I thank God he chased them away. They left with all our Lion King CDs and it made me upset because I grew up watching them. After I and my family experienced the robbery and subsequent civil war in Nigeria, my parents decided that we needed a permanent change of scenery. So, my dad suggested that we all move to the UK because of the educational benefits. My mum came to the UK before all of us. She had to complete several tests and go through many checks to make sure we would be stable. By the grace of God, everything went well, and we moved out.

Life Lesson 1

You Should Never Take Your Life for Granted

I was young, not that this is the case with everyone, but I didn't know the real meaning of life. Even now, I'm still not sure I fully grasp the importance. Sometimes, I sit on my bed and stare at the ceiling, wondering if everything in life is worth it. After a lot of introspection in recent years, I realised that the answer is 'yes' every time. I refuse to stay in the same position for the rest of my life. That's why I'm always working and learning. I have to get better because I aim to be a better version of myself every day and I suggest you do it too. I don't care how challenging the journey ahead of me is, I will face it appropriately because every day, I work hard and smart to become a new beast.

Some people think working hard is killing yourself for your craft but I don't agree. I only do what I can, and I've accepted that I'll only be able to do my best. Many gurus on social media fabricate everything. They don't show what's real, making people like you and me think we aren't doing enough and aren't enough ourselves. You're more than enough, and you'll always be. Realising that you can only do your best will save you a lot of mental and physical trouble. When I noticed this, everything got better because I stopped beating myself up over failing to follow the schedule.

Life is meant to be spontaneous and there is beauty in spontaneity because I believe that's where some of our best memories in life come from. I'm sure you have noticed that you have a better time when your day doesn't go according to the plan. Too much planning makes us lose sight of what life is meant to be, thereby affecting our personalities. Now, the way I approach my days now are different, and I think it's better too. During the day, I set a goal to complete 4-5 tasks and if I reach that goal, great. If I don't, still great. I'll simply try again the next day. Social media has somehow made everyone believe that their self-worth depends on their productivity when sometimes it's okay to just exist. I understand success is good but sometimes, take it easy on yourself. Because the number of times you slip up doesn't matter. What matters is that you get back up and keep going. Sadly, we live in a world where people kill themselves with pressure because of the negative impact social media has on their mindset.

This is why you need to be careful with what you consume on social media because all that negativity could take a serious toll on your mental health. Soon enough, you'll start thinking you aren't good enough because many people on social media say, "I will sleep when I'm dead." Whenever I see that, I shrug my shoulders because you'll find it difficult to produce anything good without being mentally and physically healthy. It doesn't matter how successful you are; if you disregard your health, then all your success will mean nothing. You must ensure your health comes before everything else. So, it doesn't matter if you take long breaks as long as you return to your pending tasks and get them done. You only work as good as your health, so prioritise taking care of yourself more, and your life will get better. While you're taking care of yourself, try to push your limits by putting yourself in uncomfortable situations until they become comfortable. It's an easy technique that has helped me grow over the last couple of years.

Also, ensure you control your social media usage too; a lot of people let their phones use them instead of the other way round. Unfortunately, social media harbours good liars who make everything seem perfect so the people that look up to them will think their life needs to be perfect too. Life will never be perfect, and that's okay. You'll never have life 100% figured out and that's one of the many beautiful things about being alive. Not having life figured out is good because it shows you there's always space for improvement. You just have to try to do better than you did yesterday and build it up from there.

If you feel like you are suffering from too many

unnecessary expectations on social media, unfollow or mute 80% of the people you're following. It'll make your life better because seeing the crap they post is not benefiting you. After you do that, follow some positive pages and sort out your feed so you'll see only positive, uplifting content. Currently, I try my best to be as real as I possibly can because I know many people look at my platforms, and they look up to me too. I don't want to ever paint a perfect picture for anyone, so I usually tell my followers about the things I struggle with from time to time. I don't want them to ever think they'll never slip up because everyone slips up eventually. The most important thing about slipping up is making sure you get back up and use what you've learnt from your previous battles to win your next ones.

This life lesson also teaches you that life is beautiful, so create meaningful friendships and relationships. Smile and laugh while you can. Value the ones you love and tell them you love them and are proud of them every day. You must have noticed that whenever you have fun with the people you love, you are usually full of life and joy. This is because you are doing what is essential and you are doing it with who you love. Life is a beautiful gift and we are all here to do something. Chase your dreams because even if it sounds crazy inside your head, it doesn't matter. Once you have thought about it, you have completed the first step of execution. The next step is going out there and putting in the work to make that dream come through. When you're putting in the work and moving towards what you want in life. You should never let the internet and social media affect you from living your life. You don't see what's going on behind the camera or posts, and I can assure you everything isn't perfect.

Chapter 3

A Fresh Start, *2008-2010*

It was January 2008. It was going to be my first time on a plane and I was scared. I had never travelled anywhere or met new people before so I was anxious. Once I figured the plane ride might be an interesting one, I refused to fall asleep. This is a habit I perfected right from when I was a child. It's not entirely a bad thing because my mother nicknamed me 'Kerosene' because I never run out of energy. Chances are that I was daydreaming about life in the UK. Eight hours later, we arrived and everything was different. The airport was cleaner and the environment looked better too.

It truly felt like I was in a foreign and new land and it was a beautiful feeling. When we left the airport, we didn't have a place to stay, but my mother had friends who lived in the UK. So we ended up staying with one of our aunties and I'm still not sure how we all managed to fit in the house. There were about five or six of us at the time, including my aunt and her children, but we made it work for about two months until we got our own house. At the time, I was attending DeLucy

Primary School, which is in Abbey Wood.

Everything in the UK was better than what I had experienced in Nigeria, including education. The rooms were cleaner, and it felt like all students had a decent relationship with the teachers. I experienced many negative situations at DeLucy, especially bullying. Many people looked at me funny because of the four tribal marks I have on my face and it brought me down all the time. They mocked my accent and called me all sorts of names due to my prominent forehead. They also called me a 'freshie.' I tried many ways to fit in with others but nothing worked. I eventually accepted that I was never going to fit in, and there is nothing wrong with that. Life is better when you turn your back against the crowd and walk down your own path. You win more as you realise that 50% of the people there are fake too. The bullying stopped after a while because they noticed that it was hard to get a proper reaction out of me. Socially, I was great but in academics, I wasn't the best. I wouldn't necessarily call myself 'smart' because I've never enjoyed education thoroughly. I was only doing it so my parents would be proud of me.

The only subject that was entertaining to me was PE because we played football all the time. I fell in love with Manchester United when I watched them play when I was two. Back home in Nigeria, we used to watch football all the time as a family. Three of my other siblings support Manchester United, my older brother supports Chelsea, and my mother supports Arsenal. My dad was not too interested in sports like the rest of us but he'd still watch and engage. Football nights were memorable as we would all sit around my Grandmother's living room and have a good time. And it was during those moments that I fell in love with Manchester United because they were winners. They were one of the top 5 teams in the world and I still remember most of the players back then.

My favourite player to watch while growing up was Ruud Van Nistelrooy. He's easily one of the best finishers I've ever witnessed to touch the football pitch. Manchester United used to win all the time, so I was usually happy. Every team feared visiting Old Trafford because they knew it would be a long 90 minutes. But every good thing comes to an end and that's why we aren't dominating football right now. However, due to my lack of interest in other subjects, my eyes started looking elsewhere. It wasn't too long until I started getting involved with girls. If my friends read this, they would laugh because they know about my stories with girls.

The first time I kissed a girl, I was nine and in year 4. Although it was a rather exciting moment, it got me into trouble because it happened in front of everyone on the playground. When I got home and my parents found out what I did, my arms almost fell off my body. That was the first time I got into trouble at school. After that happened, I realised that I had drawn attention to myself in DeLucy and since we moved into our own house, I had to move schools to St. John Fisher in South Thamesmead because it was closer than Abbey Wood.

Many of my positive and negative experiences came from moving schools. I got into many fights for various reasons. I remember one fight I got into, which started while I was waiting for my sister to finish school. Her school was opposite mine, and my mum always told me to wait for her so she could walk my younger brother and I back home. As I waited patiently for my sister, a mixed-race boy started bullying my brother. I instantly intervened and tried to beat him up but it didn't work out well. Moments later, my head was on the floor.

I ended up in the hospital with my mum and it made her angry because she had to leave work. I remember her telling me that I should act like I was in severe pain so the doctors would come to me first. It was challenging to do that because I was feeling fine. We waited in the hospital for 6 hours until the doctor saw me. He declared me fine but advised that I do not put too much strain on my mind. For the next couple of days, I didn't go to school because the punch I received from that guy left my head swollen. Experiencing this pain was the first time I concluded that nothing good comes out of anger.

Back then, my knowledge of life was limited as I used to think that you can instantly win a fight whenever you get angry. I was very wrong. Firstly, if you fight while you're angry or try to do anything productive in that state of mind, you will get it all wrong because your mind isn't clear. After the days went by, I returned to primary school and I had a great time. My favourite time was golden time on a Friday because all my friends got the chance to play football. Whenever there's an opportunity to either play or watch football, I never miss it.

Playing football made all my problems go away and the love I have for it will never go away. I wasn't the best at football during primary school and my ability was not encouraging but my love for the sport made me carry on regardless. My primary school even qualified for a tournament. I still remember the excellent AstroTurf pitch we played on back then, when we got through to the quarterfinals. Many talented footballers attended my primary school and this improved our chances to make it through. Our next opponents were tough—St. Margarets in Thamesmead.

On paper, they were better than us by a mile, but that didn't stop us from taking the game to them. We played beautiful football, but unfortunately, I got injured. I didn't want to come off, but on second thought, maybe if I had, we would have won the game. It cost us a decisive goal because I couldn't track my man since my hamstring was tight. I was stubborn. Once that tournament ended, year 6 started preparing to leave since they were scheduled to complete their program in a couple of weeks. Since it was to be the last week, it's traditional that disco will be held at the primary school.

At the time, I had a girlfriend and her name was Chantel. She was a nice girl but the problem was that I always made terrible decisions when it came to women, and you'll realise that soon. Chantel had even stopped speaking to me before the disco because of something I did. But the disco was enjoyable as I remember everyone loved JLS back then and everyone's favourite song was "Beat Again." Throughout the whole disco, I was either singing to JLS or trying to dance like Michael Jackson because he was so cool. Then, if you didn't listen to his music during primary school, you would probably be considered weird. The disco lasted for three hours and I finally went home.

Leaving primary school was a big step for me because I was moving onto secondary school. I've never been academically bright, as I mentioned earlier. Most people call me smart now because I read books. However, that's not the case. I'm wise and my life experiences have taught me the distinction between right and wrong and I continue to learn every day. Primary school was amazing. It was where I met the first person in my friendship group - AJ Oluwasina. We have been brothers for 12 years, and we will be brothers forever.

Life Lesson 2

Words Are Words, Do Not Let Anyone Stop You From Chasing Your Dreams

Everyone talks simply because we all have different opinions on things. It doesn't matter if someone leaves you a hate comment on the internet or if they give you hate in real life. Not everyone will like you. People even hated Jesus, the most spotless person to have lived on Earth. If anyone hates on you, I can assure you there is something wrong with them and not with you. They are taking time out of their day to come to your platform to spread negative energy, and that doesn't sound like something the average person would do. You should even start seeing hate as progress. They are talking about you, and your name is going around. You can feed off it if you capitalise upon the attention and channel it into something specific. Some people often hate or dislike you because they're hurting inside. This means there is a problem with them and not with you. That's how a fair number of human beings operate. On that note, I plead with you to not stop being yourself because some people don't like it. Being yourself is the best thing you can do because no one else is like you. You'll struggle to change at their pace and there's nothing wrong with being different. In fact, it's even better than being like everyone else.

If you want to change, then ensure you only change when it is what you really want and not what someone else wants. I understand some people can change you for the better, however some people want to change you just to suit their own needs and that should not be possible. If you're going to change someone just to fit your needs, it isn't natural. They will return to how they were before overtime, and that'll cause issues within your relationship with that individual.

Another reason why you shouldn't listen to hate or judgement from others is that you would probably regret it in the future. You will be in your room with your family, then you will suddenly think about that time you didn't do something you wanted to do because someone online called you ugly or not funny. So what? Everyone is ugly to someone. We all might not be funny to someone too. And that is why you should stop letting other people's words affect you, their input in your life doesn't mean anything especially if they're not your friend. You need to understand that people will always find something to talk about you whether you're doing good or bad. So do what you need to do and make sure you don't harm yourself or anyone else in the process.

Chapter 4

Mirror on The Wall, *2010-2015*

Secondary school was arguably the weirdest five years of my life. My secondary school was only ten minutes away from my house and if I was ever late, it was usually because I was up all-night taking care of my mum when she falls asleep downstairs on her favourite chair or playing PS3 with my friends.

Secondary school was weird because that's when I started going through puberty. There were many occasions where I couldn't understand what was happening with my body. I couldn't ask anyone because my dad lived in Nigeria and visited us once every year. And my eldest brother went to a university outside of the UK. So, the only person I had was my immediate older brother. I spoke to him about it a few times, but you can only do so much with advice. You have to learn about many things by yourself so eventually, I stopped asking him to help me. Maybe seeing my dad more would've helped the situation but unfortunately, I only saw him once or twice every two years.

My dad isn't to blame for this situation, nor is my mother. My mother has been working for 35 years of her life, and she's still working today. So I could barely speak to her about things too because while I was growing up, there would be times where I wouldn't see my mum for few days because of her balancing several jobs to put food on the table. It was so frustrating to watch because even though she was working a lot, it seemed like there was no money to show for it. The one thing I did growing up was always trying to see if I can make her life more comfortable. Whenever she worked, I would usually be at the house with Femi Opedo, another member of my friendship group.

Because we live literally 30 seconds away from each other, we used to go to school together and that's how our friendship got stronger. As schoolwork intensified, I began struggling with all of my subjects. When I began, I was in the best classes in everything but that didn't last too long as I couldn't keep up with the workload due to a lack of interest. But I cherished my time in secondary school because I met some of my closest friends at St Pauls Academy.

Having a lot of friends means having a lot of birthday celebrations and it was always tough asking my mum if I could go. It was so difficult to ask because I knew she was struggling. Even though she tried her best to hide it back then, I saw it. So, when my friends invited me, I would politely turn down their invitation, not because I couldn't go but because my parents didn't have the money at the time.

So, friends, if you're reading this right now, sorry for lying to you. Life was callous back then, but I thank God that things have improved for my family. We were a struggling family and what we went through has made me appreciate everything I have right now. It has also made me realise I want more in life because I want to take care of everyone I care about and give back to my community.

I want more in life because my family have never had it easy. In fact, there were times when we couldn't afford to fix our water pipes. We had to boil water in the kitchen downstairs or go to our neighbour's house to shower. I'm glad all of this happened because it has taught me how to treat what I have now better. I realised that I should never take anything for granted because tables can always turn. I could be up today and down tomorrow. I have to be grateful all the time regardless of my current situation. My mother used to complain a lot back then and it was understandable. But now, whenever she complains, I simply sit next to her and tell her, "Mum, look at how far we have come as a family. If we experienced worse situations before and it got better, then the same thing will happen again."

You should adopt this practice for your life too. Make it a point of duty to always look back to see your progress. It doesn't matter how big or small that improvement is, the fact that you're moving forward is the most important thing. Don't look back and beat yourself up over what you could have done differently. The harsh reality is that you didn't do it. All that matters is the present and thinking accordingly for your future. The past is only there to remind you of where you were before.

While getting settled in school, several months went by, and I was getting better academically. But I was still getting bullied daily. The comments didn't change much from those I received in primary school. Most people used to say, "You're African," "Fresh off the boat," "You've got a drawback" (referring to my head shape), "You've got tribal marks," and much more. Sometimes it made me cry. Subsequently, I started hating my tribal marks. I used to wonder why I had them especially when it brought me so much pain, but now I love them. I can honestly say I love myself too. I was just confused because I was being verbally attacked by children similar to me. It made no sense, but after a while, I got used to it.

As I advanced in secondary school, I realised growing up in south east London was a weird experience. Many people were selling drugs, dying left, right and centre. I was always cautious and made sure I didn't attract any attention to myself. I grew up in Thamesmead, one of the worst areas in London. Now I'm currently 21 years old, and it's better than it was when I was growing up. Thamesmead was bad because of the number of gangs in the area between 2010-2012. Several times, I was asked if I wanted to make 'quick' money. It was tempting at the time, but I said no. My mother taught us to recognise good and evil and she always emphasized that "No matter what situation I'm in, don't be afraid to ask me for money".

I respect my parents, so there was no way I was going to attempt making quick money. I'm not one to judge and I understand we all have different circumstances, but that wasn't for me. Despite being a dangerous area, south east London was a beautiful environment to grow up in. There were many fantastic footballers around my area, especially in my school. Even when school opened at 08:15 am, I'd go in at 7:00 am so I could play football in the morning. Everyone in my school called it "morning football" and it was such a good, competitive way to start the day. I couldn't fully enjoy myself because I couldn't afford indoor football trainers at the beginning of secondary school so I had to use my school shoes.

I didn't mind because as long as I was playing football, I was happy. When I was 12 years old, I decided that I wanted to play football professionally and my favourite footballers were Ronaldo (the long-retired Brazilian striker), Cristiano Ronaldo, Wayne Rooney, Ronaldinho and Lionel Messi. Watching them play inspired me, but I lacked the drive and the ability to take football seriously at that age. That didn't stop me; it made me want it more. I remember how I used to play in my back garden. I practised everything I could but unfortunately, it didn't last for too long. I was kicking the ball over the fence too much and breaking my neighbour's stuff. Then my mother complained too much about it, so my younger brother and I played less. Regardless, there were many opportunities to play football in our area that were easily accessible too.

There was one time my brother, my family friends and myself went to another secondary school in South Thamesmead to play a football tournament. At the time, I was eleven or twelve, so that means I was in year eight. We arrived at the location and had to wait. Then the coordinators told us we could pick our own teams. I thought about it and decided to be a captain, and my team members were the people I came with and a couple of others who looked good. A couple of minutes later, we started playing football and we were doing really well. Maybe it was the chemistry we had or because we used to play with each other regularly. It just felt right. Sadly, we didn't win that many matches.

My favourite position was striker because I loved scoring goals. I didn't have a good shooting technique and that's one of the main reasons why my team lost the tournament. Another reason why we lost was because while we were playing football, I was bad-mouthing a couple of other boys. It wasn't like I was doing it for no reason. They were insulting my younger brother and calling him fat. That made me angry because he has always been bullied because of his weight, especially in primary and secondary school. So when they started bullying him, I retaliated and defended him. It began to get heated, but the coordinators stopped everything because the tournament was still on. Since we were out of the tournament and had no more matches to play, we were advised to wait for everyone else to finish until we could leave the venue.

When all the matches ended, the boys continued arguing with us from the other side of the large pitch until they came to speak to my brother and me directly. They carried on insulting him, and I was defending him while tears poured down my face (I usually cry whenever I'm angry). But the coordinators came towards us again and broke up the altercation and told everyone to go home. My younger brother and my family friends went home using public transport. I decided to walk home because I didn't have my bus pass. Walking home alone was a stupid idea but I didn't have many options. Instead of walking along the road, I was walking alone along a long bridge. It's important to note that I was still crying at that point.

Then suddenly, I saw one guy walk up the stairs in front of me. I turned around slowly and saw two others behind me. I didn't run because all of my escape routes were blocked by them and I couldn't jump over the bridge. The boys got closer to me and the two from behind held my arms, restraining me, and preventing me from defending myself. The one in front punched my stomach and my face. Then they disappeared and I was left crying on the floor. While on the floor, more people walked past the road below me. Then one guy heard me and came up to speak to me. He asked me what happened, and I gave him a brief explanation. So, he helped me up and told me to go home. I was struggling to walk home due to the amount of pain they left on my head but I eventually got home. I didn't tell anyone what happened to me because they would've asked me many questions. I just went straight to my room so I could sleep. The following morning, I woke up and went to school. Unknown to me, the news of me getting in a fight had spread like wildfire. Many people told me I was lucky I didn't get seriously injured. They said this because I was smack-talking the gang members. This shocked me so I decided to keep a low profile for a long time.

I didn't tell my mum about this incident. She saw my face when I got home that evening, and she knew something had happened but I lied and told her I got injured at football. She was persistent in finding out what really happened because she had a feeling that wasn't the truth. After a while, she stopped asking me because she couldn't get the honest answer out of me. I didn't tell her because the situation would've unnecessarily escalated into something else if I did.

After I stopped keeping a low profile, I started playing Call of Duty with my friends from school. This was the first time I discovered my love for gaming. It was fascinating how you could get lost while playing a game. Your problems disappear, and it was fantastic for stress relief too. I used to play Call of Duty for hours on end. Some days I wouldn't leave my room. I would not even eat. All I wanted to do was play games, and I didn't regret it one bit. Back then, the talk of the gaming community was Optic and Faze. They were two unique clans who revolutionised the game by bringing tricks into it. They broke the rules, changed them and made the game more enjoyable. I used to spend hours watching their videos and learning how to do what they do. Eventually, I began picking up their moves a bit more. I was not as good as them, but it was good enough.

While I was playing, I realised that consistency in ONE thing is the key to proficiency in that specific thing, So stop wasting your time trying to do multiple different things especially if you aren't good at all of them.

Mini Life Lesson: Focus On One Thing Instead of Juggling More Than You Can Handle

Focus on one thing, keep it simple and trust me, you will win forever. I don't know why society thinks being busy and a serial multi-tasker is cool but you can be busy for 24 hours and get minimal work completed. On the contrary, you can use your time wisely for three hours and complete all the tasks on your to-do list. You need to realise that more complications only create more problems. Simplicity is key and it'll get you far in life. For example, we live in a society that is obsessed with multiple streams of income. They don't realise that it's gradually killing them, and that's why some people produce mediocre work. No one is perfect, and you can't be good at everything, so instead of focusing on how you can make £100,000 while doing six completely different things. Find something you love and focus on it. Thanks to social media, you can monetize whatever you love. There are many apps available for that today, and more apps will be released. We all watch random stuff on YouTube, so why not create videos on how much you love sewing? It might seem boring to some people, but you'll attract the right audience down the line.

Multiple streams of income have suddenly made some people investors too. They might have been influenced by statements like "If you don't invest, you will not be wealthy." But have you ever asked how these people are so sure that all this investing will put them in a better position in the future?

Nothing is guaranteed. You don't need to invest in anything, you don't need to have multiple streams of income from different businesses. I know people who are involved in real estate, cryptocurrency, forex trading and much more. I think they're just killing themselves slowly for no reason and they wonder why they can't keep up with their lives and live comfortably. You need to understand that history has a very high chance of repeating itself. How many times have you seen people who work multiple jobs earn less than someone who is working one? It's very confusing when you think about it, right? It's because the system has boxed everyone in with this 'minimum wage' factor and made everyone think that's the least you can earn from doing every job. That's why they never show you the highest paying salary within your field whenever you're at an interview. They want to keep you average and hinder your growth, but you can get paid way more than that. All you need to do is focus on your craft, dig deep into it and try your best to hit the jackpot within it too. When you hit that jackpot, carry on digging because it'll put you in a higher position within your career. It'll put you there because while you're digging, there's a good chance of you getting naturally better at your job. However, if you still feel like you need multiple streams of income, then I've one good technique for you.

An easy way to gain multiple streams of income while doing what you love is by being good at your job. For example, if you love going to the gym, and you made good progress in gaining weight, you can start YouTube, Instagram and TikTok. I understand some of you might not be comfortable with putting your face online. But you don't even need to put your face in your gym videos, you can simply blur it out or only record your body but alternatives to this are podcasts and blogs. If you're satisfied with all of them, I would also suggest putting your work on Snapchat and LinkedIn too. Over time, it'll only get you bigger, and when you get to a good level, and your content starts getting monetised, you'll be smiling and laughing because that's one stream of income. Another stream of income is making a weight gain plan or a weight loss plan, it'll benefit those watching you. Take your time to execute the plan, show your results and show the results of those who purchased your program. Sell it online and watch how much you'll excel, now that's two. I'm sure you can see where I'm going with this.

My reasoning for this is simple; many people are jumping into investing and much more with no sense of direction. They are only following the flock because it's 'cool' that everyone is investing now. That's how they put their money in danger. I suggest only doing it if you completely understand what you are doing. I know you might not want to miss out, but that isn't going to happen because life is all about opportunities. Don't invest or do anything for the simple fact that others are doing it and because you think it'll make you rich in the future. That can make you desperate and make you lose everything you put in. Don't feel bad because most people are investing now because other opportunities will arise and when they come, learn about it, take your time and be careful before you act. If you're stuck in this trap, focus on your self-awareness because the moment you get to know yourself better, you'll notice you can't be good at everything. Someone will always be better than you, and that's fine.

Chapter continues...

As my love for video games increased, my grades started to slip and soon enough, I had to move into a lower set in all of my classes. However, that didn't stop me from playing because I was unserious. In fact, I interpreted the demotion as enough free time to play. But all good things must come to an end.

There was one night I had to be in school by 8 am the following morning but by 4 am, I was still wide awake, shouting to my friends through the PS3 microphone. While that was happening, my dad was at my room door, watching me. I was oblivious because of how loud my headset was. Then boom, my PS3 turned off. He picked it up and threw it down the stairs and shouted at me. He told me to go to sleep, and that was the beginning of the end for my console.

I couldn't complain. My dad had bought it for my brothers and I for Christmas and it was his own money. Although it still worked after, my brother tried to cross over the wires once, it dropped, and that's when it stopped working for good. It was tough to take back then because I didn't have a console anymore but there is a lesson to be learned from this. The lesson is whatever you're doing in life – it doesn't matter if you're a teacher, lawyer, student or anything else – make sure you're all in. I don't believe in the saying, "Good things come to those who wait." If you believe in that, you'll be waiting for the rest of your life.

I believe in "Good things come to those who go out and earn them." You have to put in the work. It increases the chances of you getting your lucky break. I'm not a big fan of luck, but the harder you work, the luckier you get. You don't know who is watching you. You don't know what opportunities are opening up. The work you do in the dark will come to light. It all pays off at the end of the day. So, keep going and never stop.

After my dad caught me playing PlayStation in the early hours of the morning, school life continued naturally. I attended all my classes and regular football sessions at Charlton Athletic Football Club on Saturday evenings. It was the best. It was so enjoyable and there were barely any problems.

Two years went by and it was November 2012, and on one fine morning, I was walking into school when everyone started looking at me and laughing. I was confused, wondering if I did something wrong and nobody told me. While walking past the ICT Suite, there was one computer playing, and everyone was standing around it. There I was, on the screen. Singing my heart out. I was singing 'Mirror on the Wall' by Lil Wayne and Bruno Mars. I was suddenly hit with a flashback. I completely forgot about recording this video. It was two years old at the time it resurfaced amongst my peers. My younger brother and I attempted to upload it. However, our internet was slow so we just left the laptop there. It ended up uploading by itself. You can still watch the video on YouTube if you type in "Ursino Obamudi". Back then, I didn't want anyone to watch the video, but now I don't care. It was a good memory that I will cherish forever. But the way we got bullied for this video was ridiculous. The whole school was talking about the video for a very long time and they didn't stop until year 10.

After that incident, nothing much happened during my last two years at secondary school apart from my last exams in year 11. I didn't revise for any of my exams, but I finished secondary school with 5 GCSEs but unfortunately, I failed science. During my time at secondary school, I met more people who are still in my friendship group today. Their names are Tobi Hassan, Femi Opedo, Ayomide Adeyanju, Adam Sylla, Daniel Yaroson, Evans Okungbowa-Fuerte, Emmanuel Osaro, Ademola Osinowo, Kemi Awoleke, Asher Hines, Brain Enninful, Reuben Chumpuka, Jospeh Nganje, Kieran Murray and Sean Karuru. Most of my friendships are low maintenance, and I feel like they work well like this because we all have things to do. They have all been blessings in my life and I'm grateful we met each other.

Life Lesson 3

Controlling Yourself is Vital

When life starts to test you, you need to ensure that you're in control of your emotions. It's easier said than done, but the moment you work on your self-control, controlling your feelings becomes easier. Always remember that anger doesn't solve anything, it only creates more problems. Think before you act because every action can either change your life for better or worse. You don't want to say or do something and regret it after. Stay far away from bad energies because that is one of the main things that could affect your mood. That kind of energy can be born from anything. For example, if you feel like your friend is pulling you down, talk to them about it and advise them to change. If they don't listen, then you should distance yourself from them.

Whatever you consume externally will affect you internally, so work on your bad habits too. The reason why we struggle with controlling ourselves is that our bad habits tend to play with our emotions. If you know something you're doing is terrible and isn't uplifting you, try your best to stop. I know it's easier said than done because personally, I can't count how many times I've told myself I would stop doing this and that and the next week I find myself doing it all over again. It can be a vicious cycle. Unfortunately, that is life and avoiding it will only make it worse. Getting comfortable and tackling it makes it better.

You'll fail many times when you're trying to change but don't let that put you down. Rise above the challenge and keep going every day, and you'll get there when the time is right. Whenever I try to stop a bad habit, one technique that seems to work well for me is swapping my bad habits with good habits. Instead of physically and mentally harming myself, I take deep breaths, then go towards my bookshelf and pick up a book. Using this approach might work for you too, so feel free to let me know if it does. Most of your habits can only be controlled from your mind. For instance, your brain has been used to you smoking for nine years so that's why it's so easy for you to buy a packet of cigarettes. So, whenever you think about stopping, the voice in your head will usually say, "You've been doing it for this long, and you should continue." But the moment you change it around for a good habit, your brain has picked up how you feel when doing an uplifting activity. Now the voice inside your head will tell you positive things that'll eventually cancel out bad habits.

If you're still struggling to stop whatever is pulling you

down, then make sure you seek professional help or talk to someone in your family. You don't have to fight your habits alone because you can speak to someone you trust. Talking to them will always make you feel better and if you're lucky, you might even find someone who can relate. Don't feel embarrassed and give it a try. If you don't feel comfortable talking to your family then you can email me (you'll find my email at the end of the book). I'll reply and we can keep helping each other. Always have this at the back of your mind: if you can't control yourself, then you can't control anything. When you have proper self-control, everything around you are easier to handle. Change will never be easy; sometimes changing our clothes in the mornings can easily turn into a herculean task but don't let that discourage you. It'll be very uncomfortable at first but eventually, you'll get comfortable.

Try your best to utilise my advice but understand that you're not perfect and you'll slip up many times. I even fall back to my bad habits sometimes but I always ask myself if it's worth it before I do it. The answer is always NO and it makes me realise that whatever happens, the benefits will always outweigh the consequences.

Chapter 5

From A Boy To A Man, *2015-2017*

Honestly, I'm still surprised that I made it this far in life. Why? Because of how little I seem to care for my own life. From when I was nine till I clocked nineteen, I've always winged it. The thing about life is that your luck doesn't last forever. There will be a time when life will hit you in the face. That's when your second life begins because you've now realised that you only have one shot at this, and you'll need to take yourself seriously to make the most out of it.

I spent two lovely years at College because every single day was another opportunity to have the best time of my life. During College, my football abilities were at an all-time high. I played for two teams - Danson Sports and Erith and Belvedere. Erith and Belvedere was a terrible experience because I was usually late for my matches and it wasn't a good look. This led to me having less playing time, and eventually, I didn't play for them anymore. I played central defensive midfielder because of my build and I enjoyed dictating the play when I had the chance to. Being 6'4 made it easier for me to control this position because it was challenging for my opponents to knock me off the ball. But It's a shame that my time at Erith and Belvedere was short-lived. The only reason why I stopped playing for them was my tardiness. I always went to bed late the night before matches even though I knew I had to travel a long distance, especially on away days. After my time finished at Erith and Belvedere, I signed for Danson Sports but it was never serious. I played with most of my friends, and it was a funny experience. It made no sense how we didn't win that many games together. But we didn't care because we only played for them to get footage for my friends PE coursework.

After a while, I stopped going to training and matches because of how bad the team was. It wasn't enjoyable paying subs (monthly payments to play for the team) and losing every game.

Because I was playing less football, college became my main priority and it was very easy. I didn't find the work hard at all and I completed all my assignments to a good standard days before the due date. In college, I started talking to girls properly even though they would all reject me whenever I tried to go a bit further with them before. My experience with girls was different in college because I had become more confident. I spoke to several girls but honestly, all I wanted was to lose my virginity. I was persistent in losing it because it was one of the main conversation topics around boys when I was in college. It finally happened when I was 17. Although I would consider it an interesting experience, I now see why God told us to keep the unmarried bed undefiled in the Bible. However, I don't regret it. I have learned to live a life full of no regrets, so that way I see everything as lessons. So, if you're reading this and you're a virgin, cherish it. It's a beautiful thing. Don't feel like you're an odd one out. Please don't lose it so you can fit into society. If you want to lose it, it's entirely your choice but trust me when I say this; you're not weird because you've not done it yet. Don't let society tell you that.

Weeks went by and I continued speaking to more girls. I have no idea how many I've talked to so far but I can remember a few with whom I've had great conversations and some level of chemistry. Because I was too focused on satisfying my lustful desires than building something strong, I made several wrong decisions. I eventually lost sight of what's important in regards to women and relationships. Many women treated me wrong, but it made sense since I always found myself attracted to the wrong type of women. Due to the pain I felt from being cheated on several times, I wanted revenge, and I inflicted pain on more girls. They didn't deserve that, and the revenge didn't make anything better. It only made it worse. This section of my life taught me that if you seek revenge, dig two graves because you'll go down with them one way or another.

I stopped speaking to girls for a while because I wanted to focus on myself. College carried on as usual and there were only three things I used to do - playing blackjack or checkers in the common room, watching anime up until the early hours of the morning knowing I had school the next day and playing football on Sunday or going to support my friends at their local teams. I was an average player during this time, and I wanted to see how far it would take me. I even emailed many semi-professional teams asking them if I could come down for an open trial. One of them got back to me and told me my trial was on a Wednesday after school. The following week came and it was finally Wednesday. I was practising what I could in my back garden so I was feeling confident. School closed by 2 pm and that was when I checked the distance from Sidcup to Eastbourne. I remember seeing 2-3 hours and feeling disappointed because I expected it to be closer. I didn't end up going because of the distance, I could have travelled, but when it came to football, distance was a real problem. But when it came to girls, I used to make trips. One time, I travelled over two hours on the train to visit this girl; her name was Esther.

On the train, all I was thinking about was getting to my destination. I liked this girl a lot because we got along well and our conversations weren't forced. She didn't like me when we started speaking to each other but I had a feeling I could get her to because she was flirting back with when we were talking. We used to talk every single day for 6 months straight and that is how long it took before she admitted she had feelings for me. It was going well for a while and we were excited about starting our little relationship at that time but unfortunately, things didn't work out. Maybe the time was wrong, but I don't believe in "right person, wrong timing" because if it was the right person, then everything will work out fine. So we stopped talking completely in April 2017, with my birthday coming up in May. I didn't let it affect me because I had a strong feeling we would talk to each other again.

As my 18th birthday drew closer, my anxiety increased. I decided for my own sake that I would not do much on the day. But my mum decided it was essential that we celebrated it. In the early hours of my birthday, I was struggling to fall asleep so I stayed awake. I was in bed, pressing my phone when someone randomly sent me a friend request on Snapchat. Her name was Jennifer. I accepted it and we started talking and then I found out she knew Esther. I didn't see this as a problem. Knowing her, she wouldn't mind if I speak to her friend, mainly because we were no longer dating. One part of me wanted to continue talking to Jennifer and not tell her and I listened. We continued talking, but I felt guilty. Everything was eating me inside. I even got the chance to tell Esther because one of their other friends asked if I spoke to Jennifer. I told her the truth, but Jennifer got angry at me and she denied it.

What made this whole situation worse is that Esther

messaged me on my birthday too and I was talking to both of them at the same time. When my birthday ended, the conversation with Esther stopped and my only focus was Jennifer. I was eager to meet her and she finally agreed to see me after she finished college. We met for the first time in June 2017 and we got along well. We continued meeting each other after that until she stood me up once. It was a rainy Friday and we planned to meet up after college; I arrived on time, walked around and waited for about two hours - maybe even three. I called her severally but she didn't pick up. I messaged her after I left her about 5 missed calls and that is when she told me her Aunty had to go to the hospital. She also said it was a severe case and the ambulance came to pick her up. At this time, I was angry because she could have at least sent me a message. Her reason was valid, so as time passed, I struggled to forget it but it just didn't sit well with me. My gut was telling me that she lied but I didn't mention it to her because I knew I was going to find out soon.

Amid all of this, my time at College came to an end in July 2017. Thankfully, I finished my course well with a final grade of DDD (Distinction, Distinction, Distinction), which meant I could go to an outstanding university. I didn't end up going to a university that would suit me because I lacked common knowledge in 2017 and that led to me making a serious mistake. The mistake I made was that I didn't listen to my teachers who advised me to research universities and attend open days because it would allow me to see the university's environment and decide whether it would suit me, but I didn't go to anyone. To be honest, I didn't care that much about anything at that age, I was too laidback and because of that, I went through clearance at the University of Wolverhampton.

I ended up picking Sports Science because I studied that during college and I believed it would make university easier for me. In August 2017, I found myself working before university to earn some extra change and kill time too. Time ended up going by very fast and it was finally the night before I moved in.

Life Lesson 4

Before You Do Anything In Life, Educate Yourself About It

You don't want to make the same mistake I did. I used to think learning is such a drag. Sometimes I still do but as I grow older, I am noticing the benefits. Growing up, I never educated myself about anything, and this led me to make some of my life's worst decisions. I didn't listen to my teachers when they told me to revise and that affected my grades and reduced my choices of what courses I could study. I wanted to study Physiotherapy at first in university but I couldn't because I got a D in science. A couple more hours invested into science would have gotten me a C. I don't regret the choices I made because they got me to where I am today.

Please use this small section of my life to help you in yours. If you're going to do anything in life, please educate yourself before you take action. We're currently living in times where information about nearly everything is available within seconds. You can teach yourself how to become anything credible through Google and YouTube. With the internet, you can gain great skills that will aid you during your lifetime and leave a huge positive impact on your life. I'm not randomly telling you this, I am speaking from experience. I've been using YouTube to learn everything for the past 10 years of my life. It got to a point that people used to ask me "How did I get so good at editing videos and graphic designing?" My answer was, "I've been watching videos on both during my free time for eight years."

Fair enough, it took me a while to learn and get better. However, I saved a lot of money and time too. So, the point I am making here is before you do anything, educate yourself because the system can trick you out of everything but they can't take your knowledge away from you. If you want to stay ahead within your work field, spare at least one hour during your day learning about something you enjoy. While you're trying to do this, don't make excuses about not having enough time because it all boils down to your priorities. If you've got time to go to the cinema, then you've got time to pick up a book and read it or watch a YouTube video about whatever interests you.

You can find books about anything online and if you don't want to pay for them, you can get them for free and get better at your trade. Books changed my life and I am sure they'll change yours too if you focus on reading about what interests you. That's why most things are hidden inside a book because they know people like you and I will never open it.

Books, YouTube and Google will be around forever so you can always find reliable information in minutes instead of wasting hours pointlessly on social media. Invest in yourself by learning from books and the internet because self-investment is the best form of investment you could ever make. You can never grow too much, and you can always get better.

There's always space for improvement in whatever you are doing. That's why I try my best to follow many quotes in life, and one of them is Socrates' "True wisdom is that you know nothing." I suggest you add this quote to the few you already live by and I can assure you that you'll yearn for knowledge. Knowledge is vital in whatever you're doing. How do you think all the successful people in the world stay winning? It's because they learn more about their craft every day. If you prefer real-life experiences, then go out and live. Learn from everything and apply the acquired knowledge; that's when it becomes powerful. Educate yourself, make plans to fulfil your goals and analyse the prospects of achieving your goals. Don't be afraid to change and adapt to certain things for you to get there.

Chapter 6

Trapped, *2017-2019*

When I moved into the university in September of 2017, it was a weird experience. It was my second time travelling away from home and I wasn't sure what to expect. Depending on the train you board, the journey from London to Wolves is between one to three hours. We took the longest train because the fare was a reasonable price. As I got onto the train, I couldn't stop thinking about what the environment would be like and if I was going to settle in properly. I was nervous because I had never left home before, but we finally arrived at Telford hours later. I tried looking for an accommodation close to my campus, but they were all taken. I didn't want to share a toilet with anyone, so I decided to stay in Telford. My mother helped me sort out my accommodation and bought me some food. I thought the food would last for a very long time but it finished within a week. During my first week, I met a couple of acquaintances through a WhatsApp group chat. In the UK, you enter freshers' chats and party chats before you go to university to meet new people and socialise. I barely talk in group chats, mainly because I don't use most of my social apps often. Because I refused to socialise, I could not make any proper friends. The only people I knew properly at my university was my sister and her friends and I was okay with it because not being around people helps me function better. While I waited for university to start in two weeks, I stayed inside my room watching anime or playing FIFA to keep myself busy.

From ages 13 to 16, I was terrible at FIFA. The only game I was decent at was Call of duty as I mentioned in chapter 4. I still love the game; I remember playing Modern Warfare 2 and Modern Warfare 3. I used to play for hours and sometimes, I would pretend to be sick in school so my teachers could send me home. My friends and I used to go to Ademola Osinowo's house or Adam Sylla's after school and all we did was play FIFA or Call of duty either on Xbox or PlayStation. I used to lose on FIFA but I held my weight on Call of duty. I wanted to get better at FIFA mainly because at that age, every boy used to talk about it and the competitive side of me wanted to be the best. Unfortunately, I didn't have a console, so I couldn't play.

I wanted a console so bad but I couldn't afford it. I applied for several jobs during March 2017 but I didn't get any of them. Then finally a couple of weeks into April 2017, I got a job through one of my friends. I worked for a week at Crystal Palace football club as a waiter and got enough money to buy my first PS4. When I got my PS4, I started playing pro clubs with my friends but I didn't bother playing against anyone because I knew I wasn't good enough. I had to take my time practising online before I challenged any of them. I played most matches in seasons and patiently waited till I got better. The more I played, the better I got but I was still not good enough. I was frustrated because, at that age, I expected rapid results, but nothing was improving to a great level. The reason why I wanted to get better is that I had something to prove.

In College, I used to board the 53 bus and my friends and I would usually have loud discussions at the back of the bus. This one time, I was talking to Adam Sylla and we were arguing about who is better at FIFA. To be fair, he was way better than me at that point. We had played twice on FIFA 17 and he won both matches. FIFA 18 was about to drop so I told everyone on that bus that I'd end up being better than him at FIFA 18. They all laughed at me but I knew I was going to get it done. One thing you should know about me is that if I tell you I will do something, I'll get it done. It might take longer than others but I have ultimate confidence that I will complete what I said. I knew it was going to be tough, but I didn't care because I was ready for the challenge. That seemingly playful conversation I had with Adam Sylla is a conversation I'll never forget for the rest of my life. It was the start of something great and bad and you'll soon find out why.

It was because of that flashback I just explained that I started playing FIFA religiously. My main goal? To get better. I remember playing and trying to qualify for a competitive tournament during the weekend. I never won it once during the summer holiday before university, when I and Ayomide Adeyanju used to stay awake all night playing until I heard my mother at the door because she was coming back from work. I would quickly turn off my console and run upstairs. She caught me in the act so many times and it was embarrassing every time.

From the end of college to university, all I did was play video games with no schedule and it affected my grades. I already lacked motivation because my university accommodation was two hours away from my campus. I had to wake up at 6 am every day, get ready, catch the bus at 7:30 am which gets to Wolverhampton at 8:30 am. Then wait until 9:15 for the next bus to Walsall. My lecture started at 9 am, so I was always late. I tried my best to keep up with this schedule but after a while, I stopped going in. It was too much to take and the fact I didn't enjoy Sports Science also influenced my decision. The workload was ridiculous, and due to my missing lectures, I was always confused.

I would stay in my room 24/7 playing FIFA. I barely went to any parties because that has never been my type of scenery. I have nothing against people who go to parties. Have fun and enjoy yourself. I don't do balloons, never smoked weed in my life or smoked anything else in general, although I drink occasionally. The reason why I don't do any of it is I don't see the benefits of doing it in the long term. I understand many people use it as an escape from problems or even genuinely enjoy it. What matters is how you prioritise your time. If you want to be great, then you can't spend all your time doing that stuff. It makes no sense because, in the long term, it will only slow you down. It's why most people struggle to find time to do what they love. However, this is just my opinion; if you have no problem with it, continue, but if you do, try your best to stop.

Since I wasn't going to any parties in my first year of studying Sports Science, all I did was play FIFA 24/7 or meet Jennifer. I was talking to her throughout summer 2017 but we never met each other privately but our conversations were very lustful. So over time, a lot of sexual tension built up between me and her. This is because growing up, I lacked significant self-control and I was always horny. I would guess that it was because of all the pornography I was watching; a habit that messed me up mentally and physically even though I didn't realise it at the time. Then, it used to feel normal but now, I am glad I stopped watching porn and masturbating. It was difficult at first and sometimes I fell back into the habit, but I got there in the end. If you struggle with it, please stop because it ruins all your emotions and makes you feel numb. It messes up your perception of women, makes you feel tired/unmotivated, gives you the wrong impression of sex and much more. I'm not too sure what the disadvantages are for women, but I don't think it's that beneficial for them too. I just feel like you'll enjoy having sex more with whoever you're doing it with if you quit masturbating and watching porn. You'll also feel more energetic if you refuse to be a slave to pornography. However, this is just my opinion. If you have no issue with it then, by all means, do as you please.

Due to all the sexual tension, I and Jennifer finally decided that it was time for us to meet each other again, so I travelled to her place. I got the late train to Coventry, the university she went to. I had to stop at Birmingham New Street station first and I arrived at 11:50 pm but the trains going towards Coventry stopped at 11:30 pm. This left me with two options: go back home or pay £40 to spend the night with her. I chose the second option. I still remember the cab journey like it was yesterday. I was rushing the driver to get there quickly, mainly to have sex with her. The journey was 40 minutes long and it felt like I was never going to reach my destination but I did arrive. It was a windy night and the walk from the cab to her place wasn't too long. I got there and sent her a text. In a few minutes, she came to usher me in and we watched a couple of movies until we got comfortable. Then we ended up doing everything we spoke about during summer, and the experience was interesting. I was meant to only stay for one night but I was there throughout the whole weekend. We talked a lot, got to know each other better and we watched many movies. When the weekend came to an end, I went back to Telford and back to FIFA.

As soon as I got back to Telford, my addiction to FIFA started, I would wake up at about 1 pm and play until about 3 am the next day. No university assignments were getting completed, all I was doing was playing FIFA. I was barely even speaking to people and Jennifer got angry at me because the attention I was giving to her reduced a lot. Even though we still talked from time to time, my replies became slower. It was never really a relationship but I remember it was toxic because we used to argue a lot. We would go days, sometimes even weeks, without speaking to each other. Then I would message her and ask to see her. Take her out and end up having sex throughout the night. We barely knew anything important about each other because my attention was only on FIFA and that ruined what we had. There was one time I was in the PS4 party chat with my friends. We were laughing and enjoying ourselves when a notification popped up. It was a text from Jennifer that read, "Babe, I think I am pregnant." My heart dropped. I stopped playing my FIFA match immediately and called her. She then explained to me what she was experiencing, and these were symptoms of pregnancy. I had no idea what to tell her. My mind was in scrambles. She told me she would visit the clinic to confirm if her suspicions were true. During that whole week, I barely played any games.

I struggled to sleep because all I could think about was

having a child. The following Monday arrived in November 2017 and she went to have the test at a clinic. The results came back but she refused to share them because, according to her, the doctor had thrown them in the bin. That's when I sat down on my bed and laughed having discovered that she had been lying all along. She had just sold herself out with that crappy lie and I realised she was just doing it for attention. I had always known some girls to be desperate but that was my first time having a first-hand experience.

At the end of her little pregnancy prank, our relationship went left. We barely talked and everything just died a natural death. Eventually, we stopped speaking and that was when she admitted that she had been joking about it. It was a blessing in disguise because during the summer of 2019, I worked at M&S. Someone I worked with told me he was having sex with her even when we were still together. It made me feel used and weird, but then I realised I deserved better. I even asked her and she lied about it too but the guy gave me proper evidence. I showed her the evidence and she still tried to cover up her act but I had enough, so I blocked her.

Moments after I blocked her, I messaged Esther and told her about the last year or so, and she told me she was glad I opened up about it but because I disrespected her, she didn't speak to me again after that. Looking back at it now, it was a silly mistake. But I was uneducated at the time, so I am glad that I learned from it too. You can't change the past;

however, you can change yourself to make your future better. While all of this happened, three months went by and my first assignment was about to be due, but I didn't turn it in. I attempted it but FIFA was the main thing occupying my time, every day. I'm sure you are wondering if I ever got better at FIFA. Of course, I did; I was playing well and comfortably, giving professional players a good game. I knew about the money you could make in Competitive FIFA, and that caught my eye. At the back of my mind, all I was thinking about was winning one tournament or having one of my gaming videos on YouTube go viral. So, I could live off the money.

Eventually, one video I made did numbers, but I barely had any subscribers to show for it. Maybe it was because of how confusing my channel was, but this affected me a lot long term. I was putting in hours' worth of work but I had nothing to show for it. I would stay in my room and only leave when I needed to get food. I was just in my room, lost in thoughts, feeling depressed and self-harming myself. I didn't leave my accommodation for about two weeks and my December 2017 exams were around the corner. All of that time spent playing FIFA was useless and I wasn't attending any lectures either.

FIFA took all my time because I lacked self-control, and I didn't know how to make time for myself and what is essential. On one snowy day, I had two exams. I went outside to get the bus from where it usually stops. I waited for a while but it didn't come, then I got told that the location moved to the front of the Co-op. As I was about to get on the bus, my thoughts started to creep in and get the better of me. All I could think about was, "What is the point of going? You did not prepare, so you are going to fail anyway." I listened to the voice inside my head and made my way home. I tried to get extenuating circumstances, but my case lacked evidence, and I just missed two exams. And this was the case for the rest of the year. I didn't know what was going on at university. I didn't keep up with my academic life and it affected me.

In July 2018, 6 months later, my results finally came out and I failed five out of six of my modules. My mother was right next to me and words cannot even explain the pain I saw in her eyes. All of them had said 'not attended/not submitted.' I got a good grade in just one because I studied it for six hours in the library with my sister and her friends' help. Passing one was never going to be enough because you need 120 credits to go into the next year and I only got 20. This left me with little to no option except one. My lecturers told me I could try re-sitting all my modules before August 2018. However, I chose not to. I figured that the workload was way too much for me to complete in such a small amount of time. All of this made me feel terrible because every day at university, my parents would call me. They would always ask me if I was focusing on my work and my answer was always yes.

Instead, I was inside my room, rotting away and playing games. Soon, it was September 2018 and I had already decided that I was going to re-do the year. This time, I figured it would be better because my Accommodation was in Wolverhampton next to my sister. I had some motivation there but nothing changed; I still struggled to go to lectures. I either woke up late or just missed the bus. But, I was doing my work more and to a better standard too. I was still playing FIFA, even more than the year before. I was excellent at this time. I beat a couple of known professional players and it fueled my ego. It led to me talking for no reason, thinking I was the best. So during my second attempt at studying sports science in my academic year of 2019, I was balancing assignments and FIFA but it was never going to work; one of them was going to suffer. Assignments took the hit and I barely attended lectures. That was the case for the whole year and by the time the university year finished, it was July 2019. I was in my room on my phone and my family friend sent me a picture of a tournament that JD Sports was hosting.

He said I should qualify but I was skeptical at first because I had barely played FIFA for the last three months. Even though I was too scared to sign up, my friends and family encouraged me to and I eventually did. A couple of weeks later, I had to show my skills to the world. The tournament location was in Stratford, Westfield. My friend, Ayomide Adeyanju, and I expected to play in a studio since that's the conventional way of FIFA tournaments, but we didn't. We played in the middle of Westfield where JD Sports set up a nice little hub. We walked towards the hub and I completed the registration form. The woman there told me to wait until another coordinator called me to come and play my match. A couple of minutes later, they called me, and it was game time. I remember the tournament was in a knockouts format. Only the final two from each side were going to make it to the live event in Manchester.

Knowing this, I made sure I performed well and won all of my matches including the final that got me into Manchester. I played so well that everyone was surprised at how talented I was. They even interviewed me, and I told them that over the last two FIFAs. I've played over 10,000 matches. The pundits were surprised but it made them realise why I was good. So, after all of that, they told me they would see me in Manchester. When I got home, the first thing I did was write a long paragraph about how hard it was for me to get there and posted it on Instagram. Unknown to me, that was a very big mistake and I will touch on this in life lesson 6.

While I was home, I had a few weeks until the tournament was happening to prepare. I tried preparing but I was not surrounded by people who could challenge me, so I stopped after a while. Maybe I was too confident. But it was FIFA 19, the most broken game I ever played. All you needed was information on the meta to give you a slight edge over your opponents. I played 5000 FIFA matches during FIFA 19 and

I knew the game inside out. Although I woke up early on the event day, Ayomide Adeyanju and I almost missed our train. The journey to Manchester was 3-4 hours long and when we got there, we had to find our way to the arena. As we started making our way, we were both surprised at how beautiful Manchester was.

While we both practised a few game plans, Ayomide Adeyanju tried to keep me calm and steady for the task ahead of me. 30 minutes went by and we arrived with lots of time to spare. However, I was nervous. Not nervous because I thought I wasn't good enough but nervous because it would be my first time playing in front of a huge crowd. After analysing the arena and assuring myself it was nothing serious, my nerves began to relax. I tried to imagine playing in my bedroom. It worked and soon, I was able to control my emotions. Moments later, the coordinators came over to me and the three other FIFA players that qualified out of 800. There were two from Manchester and one from London excluding me. They came over to explain the format of our matches, telling us that we were going to play over two legs. I was comfortable with it because I was already used to this format because of the number of competitive matches I have played in my career. When the coordinators finished explaining, we played rock paper scissors to see which two would play first. One person from Manchester won against me so my match was going to be second, so I had to wait for the other two competitors to play. Their match started and I analysed their game well and in terms of levels on FIFA, there was no one there on my level but in my opinion, FIFA is a game filled with slim chances and luck. As their match went on, the opponent from London who qualified with me comfortably beat his opponent over both legs and it was finally time for me to play my first match. I was already sitting down when we were advised to pick our teams quickly. I used Juventus and my opponent was using Belgium. He scored in the first half but I equalised in the second half and that means we had it all to play for in the second leg. I ended up winning the match over two legs, but it was a bit tricky; the opponent wasn't too bad and I can't remember the exact scores. I was interviewed after my game and I was cocky because I knew a lot of my friends in London were watching me play. I wasn't being the calm and composed FIFA player I usually was but I had to give them a good performance to watch. When my interview finished, we had a little break so I and my opponent could get something to drink before the final. This was my chance to make sure I was ready; I went to the toilet and prepared myself, came out and sat in my seat. Before we started playing, the coordinators introduced us to the audience and explained the rules too. Then they gave us the go-ahead and told us to pick what team we were going to use. I picked Juventus again because of Cristiano Ronaldo as he was the most broken player on FIFA 19. All I had to do was cross the ball to him and there's a 95% chance he'd score.

My opponent decided to use France, then the match began and went on for a while before he started applying lots of pressure. Because of the pressure, it was only a matter of time before he broke me down. He was playing very well and he finally started scoring many goals. I couldn't stop it and I was trying everything I knew, several tricks in the book, but they didn't work. He ended up winning the first leg by quite a margin; the second leg was no different. He won the tournament, £2000 and a trip to Las Vegas. Everyone came around him including the coordinators to interview him. While I was watching his interview, I was gutted wondering how I let myself fumble against players I was better than. Eventually, his interview finished and they were going to interview me but I left immediately and took my train back to London because I was so sad. The journey home was so frustrating, I was so disappointed.

In my head, I constantly called myself a failure for about one week. Throughout that whole week until Sunday, I kept thinking about what people would say. When I said this, I realised that FIFA probably wasn't for me because it isn't the first time something like this happened. I have lost many small tournaments, and instead of me being upset about it, the first thing I would think about is what other people had to say about me. It showed me that I was doing it to gain their approval. I was entertaining a crowd that wasn't even watching. I knew something had to change; I couldn't continue living my life for the approval of others. I started thinking about what I actually wanted to do with my life. I was still thinking on that beautiful Sunday afternoon when my phone rang.

I picked up the phone and I recognised the voice; it was one of the big coordinators from the tournament. He told me, "Why did you run off and not say anything?" and "We have been trying to contact you, so we can tell you something." I replied, "Tell me what?" to which he responded, "You came second, even though you missed out on £2000 and a trip to Las Vegas, you won £1000." There was a brief moment of silence because I was shocked. I didn't expect to win anything, so I told him, "Thank you." He cut the phone, and I informed my mother about the good news. She was so happy and started dancing even though I lost. She was happy because I tried and that, according to her, was enough. I was still in shock that I had just won £1000 because it was the first time I had received any money from playing FIFA. I didn't even know what to do with the money, so I kept it for a while until August 2019. I then decided that it was time for me to treat myself and I went on a shopping spree and bought some tracksuits and trainers.

As I was shopping, a notification popped up on my phone. It was my university results. There were finally out and I completely forgot. I checked the email and it said I passed five out of six modules. I was confused and gutted because the one I failed was the same one I failed three times in 2018.

It made no sense, I tried speaking about it to the university but I didn't make any significant progress. My university wasn't listening and then they said because I had failed twice, they had no choice but to kick me out. I emailed them to ask if I could start again on a sports-related course. They replied, "No. The only way you can continue studying here is if you change your course and start again." I was happy they gave me a solution, but I didn't know what to study. I spoke to my parents about it and they told me I should think about it properly before I make any decision. I started thinking about many possibilities and then I realised that I have loved watching business-related videos for about seven years. So I decided I was going to study business but I hadn't decided on an area. I analysed many options and finally decided I was going to study International business management because it is a broad course. I called my university the following morning and applied through clearing. I waited for a while before they accepted my offer and I was scared they would reject my application because of my academic history. It didn't ruin it. They accepted me a couple of days before the university was scheduled to resume.

Life Lesson 5

Overnight Success Is a Myth

Don't let social media fool you. Listening to people who know nothing about what they are talking about will ruin your life. I feel like social media is full of a bunch of know-it-alls that know absolutely nothing at all, giving irrelevant information, and leading most people astray.

That's why you need to be careful with the pages you follow because many of them seem to talk like success is something you can acquire overnight. I used to think the same thing when I was younger but after reading many books on this topic, I realised there is no such thing as overnight success; it takes time. Anything of great value usually takes a long time to acquire because the longer it takes you to get whatever you're after, the more you'll learn about the trade on your way up and that'll help you sustain it and grow it too. Even if you gain your success quickly, there's a high chance you might lose it because you don't know what to do with it. An example of this is people who come out of nowhere based on hype. Hype is a good thing but it really isn't special.

Haven't you noticed that every single big brand in the world is barely in the spotlight on social media? It's because we already know what they're doing and they've built their brand up to a point where the hype isn't the only thing carrying it anymore. That's what everyone should aim for. Even if you don't own a business, start treating yourself as a business because you manage yourself.

So, I am sure you're wondering if the hype won't carry what I'm doing, what's going to keep it firm and strong instead? For me, value, hard work, product (which is yourself if you don't own a business) and a proper foundation are the most important things you should aim for when trying to sustain a business for decades. If you hit all of these, you'll build a strong loyal relationship with all of your customers that'll make your brand stand firm for decades. That's why it's also important to trust your process and have your vision, not someone else's.

Be yourself, stand out and make sure you adapt to whatever life throws at you. Understand that when you go up the ladder, many people will be confused. They'll laugh at you and even call you weird. However, don't expect them to understand. You're going to a different place than them because your process is different from theirs. Please, try your best to not get frustrated too and enjoy the process throughout your whole life. See your life as a marathon and not a sprint. I'm sure many of you want the prize without the process, but it's during the process that you'll know whether you deserve the reward or not. You need to be in it for the long run and notice there are no shortcuts too.

That's why the process is fantastic. It will make you go crazy by testing you every time. Everything that goes good and bad is testing you. If it goes right, it's a test of whether you'll let that success get to your head and get complacent. The moment you notice complacency, readjust and get back to the basics. Complacency is the first step towards crashing everything you've worked for. When everything goes wrong, will you sit down and say, "Why does it have to be always me?" or will you look at your problems and find opportunities within your them? Always try your best to find paths through your problems instead of behaving like a victim because a victim mentality will hinder your progress. The moment you stop feeling like a victim is the moment you come in control.

This life lesson is simple to use because by trusting the process, you'll learn lots of lessons on how to treat your success better. You'll cherish everything when you get to the point where you're proud of yourself. An easy way to follow the life lesson is by blocking out the noise from everything that isn't adding positive value to your life. Focus on what's adding positive value and always think long term and when you finally get to the top of your ladder, don't get complacent. You need to understand that if you're worth £10 million, you can double that into £20 million and so on.

That's why it's significant that you always try to get better at your craft.

Don't be satisfied with your past achievements and focus on deep work. Don't rush the process, fall in love with the process because it never stops. An example of someone who fell in love with the process is Michael Dapaah. Before he became as big as he is now, he recorded a ridiculous number of skits for a long time before he recorded 'Man's Not Hot." That was the song that pushed his career to a new level. Looking at his life should show you that there needs to be a lot of years invested into whatever you're doing for it to scale properly. While you are putting in the work and hours, make sure you show up every day and maintain a strong level of consistency in your craft because you'll reap the rewards further on down the line.

I understand doing all of this is very hard especially if you haven't got much support from your family and friends. But, in my opinion, that's not the case. Their support is great, but can that take you where you really want to go? Odds are it will only get you known around your area. If you're not receiving support from your family and friends, don't worry about it too much. Focus on who is supporting you, communicate with them and get to know them better. Knowing them better will make you a better person, and it'll benefit your business down the line too. An easy way of getting to know your customers better is by making sure you reply to every single comment you get. We all have time to do irrelevant things that aren't benefiting us, so sparing 10 minutes out of your day to reply to your comments isn't going to harm you. Responding to them is crucial because, without the people supporting your business, it becomes worthless. You should also do it because word of mouth is easily one of the best marketing techniques. It's even better than it used to be because of how fast information can now be transferred. So, providing your customer with good customer service gives you a high chance of gaining more because they'll most likely tell their friends about you. This will benefit you tremendously because it's an easy way to grow your business while receiving constructive criticism and great support.

Chapter 7

The Last Battle, *2019-2020*

It was September 2019 and I was about to start my business course. I didn't know what to expect so I resolved to attend all my lectures to improve my odds of passing but due to circumstances above my control, I couldn't fulfil it. It was out of my control because I lacked self-control, I couldn't manage everything I wanted to do, and my social media addiction was terrible. Back then, I used to spend hours doing nothing on social media. Well, I was laughing, but that was pretty much it. That's why all my assignments were completed last minute, and I barely had time to sleep too but whenever I woke up on time, I would go to my lectures. Going made me very happy because International Business Management took me by surprise and I was enjoying it.

The thought of me enjoying university made me excited, and the excitement gave me motivation. I started attending more lectures and making sure I was up to date on work. It was very hard to stay up to date because the lecturers talked too fast and I would only catch up whenever I got home. As I continued this habit, I noticed the difference it was making in my grades. It had positively impacted them and they were slightly better than they were before. As my grades got better, I became an average student and I was getting 50% on my assignments.

I didn't complain much; it was my first time doing the course. As long as I was making progress, I was happy. I was still playing FIFA, but I played less. I eventually stopped in November 2019 for good. I sold my PS4 because the game was affecting my mental health. It made me say all kinds of bad things about people I didn't even know in real life.

After I stopped playing FIFA, my life gradually started to get better. I felt happier, and it was like a tremendous amount of weight got lifted off my shoulder. Now all I had to focus on was YouTube and university. I tried being a YouTuber before, but it didn't work. I feel like you need to have a severe drive for whatever you want to pursue otherwise, your work ethic will reduce over time. That's why I stopped YouTube and FIFA. I noticed I was only doing both so people would know I'm doing something with my life. That should never be the case. When I stopped YouTube in January 2020 for good, I was lost in life, I didn't know what to do. However, a couple of girls tried speaking to me on a serious level but I had to cut ties with them. One thing about me is I don't want to be a burden to anyone so I always ensure I'm good because if I'm doing well mentally and physically, then all of my relationships would do well too. I understand that as an individual, you will never be fully ready for a relationship but at this time, I just felt focusing on myself was more important. This is when I started working on myself around the beginning of February 2020. I tried getting into several things just to see what sparks my interest and then suddenly, one of my inspirations, Memphis Depay, announced that he was about to release his first book, "Heart of a Lion".

Since I was 12, my mother would advise me to read but I never listened. I thought it was boring, and not beneficial. But little did I know that something brilliant was about to begin in my life. It was the start of my change and fully diving into something I love. As I was trying to dive into it more, reading was a big challenge. It was hard because my attention span isn't the best. I found it very hard to read a page for more than one minute so I read on and off for a couple of weeks until it was March 2020.

When March came, a pandemic started that affected the whole world and immediately put England in a national lockdown. I didn't know what to do with myself because I knew I was going to be inside for a very long time. So I weighed my options and it was either I started reading again or I play my brothers' PS4. Fortunately, I chose reading. So I went on Amazon and bought two more books. There were *Ego Is The Enemy* and *The Obstacle Is The Way* by Ryan Holiday. I waited for a while for them to come and when they did on March the 6th, I was so excited. I had heard great things about Ryan Holiday and the work he does and I was very eager to read the book. I went outside to pick up my delivery and ended up opening it before I came back inside. I was reading the first couple pages as I was walking through my front door and I said to myself, "Buying these books might be the best decision I've made in my life so far." I said this because I was so shocked by the amount of life-changing information that one book contained. The information I was perceiving instantly hooked me to the book and I ended finishing it in April. It took me a month but it was definitely worth it. When I was done with *Ego Is The Enemy*, I decided it was time for me to move on to *The Obstacle Is The Way*. I remember it took me the whole of April 2020 to finish reading this book but I was amazed yet again.

I started thinking about how much information we would never know because we refused to open books and explore. My birthday was getting closer again (if you've been paying attention throughout this whole book, you'd know my birthday is in May). May started well but during the first 10 days, I didn't do much. All I remember doing was watching anime or playing football. The 10 days flew by quickly and it was now May 11th and time for me to get my haircut. I was excited because I had not cut my hair for a very long time, and it was the first time I was going to this barber. I had heard good things about him and was expecting him to give me a good haircut. I made my way to his shop in Elephant and Castle and the journey was nice and smooth. I had to walk a bit from where my friend parked his car but eventually, I got in and it was my turn to cut my hair. I hopped into the chair and in 45 minutes, the haircut was completed. I looked at myself in the mirror and was just full of joy. I remember taking so many videos that day due to the happiness I was feeling. I took a good amount and my friends helped me take some too but after we were all done, we went back to our area and just relaxed for the next two days. Nothing really happened during the 12th and 13th but towards midnight on the 14th, my older siblings made me pop a bottle for the first time. It was so awkward because I had no idea what I was doing but I was in the moment so I didn't think much of it. I received so many calls from my relatives all over the world, some of which I missed while I was sleeping. After a good sleep, I spent the whole day at home because of the raging pandemic. But regardless, I received a lot of love on my 21st birthday which made me realise how much people care about me.

My birthday ended and I was happy with the celebrations, however, the lockdown didn't look like it was ending anytime soon. That's why I tried my best to keep myself busy - I read a lot online and watched podcasts on YouTube until something I'll never forget happened a few weeks later in the beginning of June 2020. I was downstairs washing the dishes when a notification popped up on my phone. I checked it and it was an email from my university saying I owe them £9000.

I stopped for a second because I thought my eyes were deceiving me but I looked again and that's what it actually said.

Then I called them; they explained that the year I'm doing now hasn't been covered. I was confused because if student finance didn't pay for the year, then why did they allow me to start? Student finance usually pays £9000 to the university which covers the tuition fee. Their response left me feeling puzzled so I called my university and explained the situation to them. And they basically said the same thing. Nothing was changing and I realised I was only wasting my time, and there was no possible solution. However, they told me the only solution was that I had to pay £9000 to finish my education myself. There was no way I was going to get £9000 in about three months, especially in a global pandemic.

That's not a small amount of money. The people working in the finance department at my university emailed me and said they needed the money before September to ensure I'm eligible to continue. When they informed me of this development, I started performing so many calculations in my head. I was thinking of a possible way of getting the money myself but there wasn't. I then asked my mother for some advice and she told me "not to think about it too much." I didn't ask her for the money because she has her own life to live and handle. I had a feeling that my dad was going to get involved and I called him just to check up on him and he said

"I shouldn't worry." He told me to try my best and make sure all my assignments are good. He will get the money to pay for me. I had a bit of faith, so I was working hard on my work. It was difficult because I had that £9000 at the back of my mind 24/7, making it difficult for me to concentrate. I was also thinking about other alternatives, in case he doesn't get the money (and this is how you should treat life. Make sure you pray for the best and prepare for the worst).

I told my father not to worry about it because I didn't want to be a burden. I accept what I did in the past in the hope of seeking a better future. I am always fully accountable for my actions because I knew what I was doing at that moment, whether good or bad. I didn't want my father to bail me out. I've always preferred to suffer in silence and figure it out before I ever ask for a handout. However, he's my father, and I am his responsibility, so I guess it was different. Even when I told him not to pay, he carried on reassuring me that he was going to.

Knowing this put my heart at ease for a while and a few weeks went by. Around June 18th, I was already speaking to a girl on a serious level. I told her about the situation I was in and she helped me by reassuring me and making sure I was doing my work. Everything was going fine between us after but suddenly a couple of weeks later, we were talking on Snapchat and her replies were just…off. I had a feeling something was wrong with her and I told her to tell me what it was and she did. She said, "I want us to stop speaking."

The moment I heard this, my heart dropped; I was heartbroken. However, I didn't act out of character, her reasoning was valid. I'm not going to say it here, but I understood why. Who knows, maybe it was also because I didn't know where I was going with my life that she ended it too.

No one ever knows the truth except the actual person that said it. After she told me that, we stopped speaking completely. I found it very hard holding conversations with her and I was feeling so down. All I could think about was her and why it didn't work out. Nothing else was on my mind except that and my situation with university. One time in Emmanuel Osaro's car with Evans Okungbowa Fuerte, we started talking about life. They said they wanted to achieve great things but I said I wanted an average and mediocre life. It occurred again when I was in Sean Karuru's car and we were catching up on life. I was upset and told him that I was suffering from depression and suicidal thoughts. We had a transparent conversation about it and made me feel better eventually. I also have to thank God for the female friends I have because experiencing this whole situation without them would've been a nightmare. When I began feeling better about everything that happened between us, there was a huge positive change in my life. I completely turned my life around for the better and completed my final four assignments in two weeks. My grades went from 40% to 60% and 70%. This means I passed my first year so all that was left was settling the university. It was not until the beginning of September that my mother told me my father was about to send the money. It took me a long time to process everything that was happening because £9000 isn't an easy sum to come by and I was wondering why he would spend that money on me and not something else. But I remember that the main reason why my parents brought me to this country is to give me the life that they didn't have.

After processing everything, I was so happy because after two years of attempting to get into my second year of Sports Science, I was finally a second-year student of International Business Management and university was about to start again in two weeks.

Life Lesson 6

You Will Learn More from Failure Than Success

Success is great and it's a nice feeling. However, it's a very lousy teacher because how are you going to get better if you keep on winning? You'll only get to know what you need to improve if you fail. So start taking every loss like you're taking a lesson. Get your notebook out or even your phone. Write down everything from your perspective, look at where you went wrong and take full responsibility and accountability for what happened. Accountability is a fantastic thing but, unfortunately, so many people are quick to blame others for their problems. You shouldn't do this. Instead, always try your best to blame yourself because when you blame someone else, you're letting them dictate your life. You're giving them complete control. However, by being accountable for it, you regain control and you can therefore see where you went wrong and how you can approach it better in the future.

That's why I'm always preaching about accountability on social media. It literally changed my life. I can assure you that if I hadn't failed so many times in FIFA and I wasn't accountable for it every time, I wouldn't be as good as I am now. I wouldn't have learned anything if I had won the FIFA tournament I mentioned in Chapter 6. Losing that tournament humbled me and taught me not to be overconfident. It taught me that I shouldn't underestimate anyone, regardless of their skill level. I went into that venue with high hopes because, on paper, I was the best there. However, I was only interested in feeding my ego, which cost me the trophy. It also taught me that I should never make any public announcements. Before I used to be a big fan of announcing what I'm doing but I noticed people aren't happy for you. Many people are keeping an eye on you for both good and bad reasons. Many people would rather smile at your sadness than be happy for you. Which is why I no longer talk about my current plans. I let my results do the talking instead.

Now take a look at how much I learned from losing. I promise you it's not as bad as it seems because whenever you lose, another opportunity always opens up. So don't be afraid to lose. Instead, embrace it because it's all part of the process. When you lose, instead of anger, smile. Fall in love with losing because you will lose a lot more as life goes on.

Chapter 8

Reflection, *2021*

Wow, what a journey my life has been so far. Looking back at everything that happened to me, I wouldn't have had it any other way. Growing up, I used to always think it was bad luck but now I know my life was meant to be like this. Everything happened for a reason and all the dots had to connect for me to be where I am today. So I am grateful for all my experiences even though some caused me a lot of pain. Pain, admittedly, is sometimes the best discipline.

It has been a fantastic journey so far from Nigeria to London. I'd say the moment I've enjoyed the most during my journey is competing on FIFA. Even though it was the worst time for my mental health, it was still the best because FIFA taught me many lessons. It was honestly a pleasure to play while knowing everything was on the line and the adrenaline rush it gave me was second to none.

Besides FIFA, I also enjoy what I'm doing now, reviewing

books and telling others the best ones to read. I plan on doing this for as long as I possibly can but I would say my end goal is to make sure that my family are comfortable forever and hopefully, I will leave a beautiful legacy behind.

I also promise you that I will be one of the most influential people to ever live on earth, so remember my name. What I'm doing and what I am going to do in the future will touch and change many lives for centuries to come. I don't care about the money, cars, clothes and fame. I care about making sure I can provide proper value in whatever way I can to others because that's what it's all about since giving back is key. Nothing makes me happier than knowing that I have had a positive influence on someone else's life. So I'll continue breaking down barriers and doors and showing everyone the way towards success, fulfilment and happiness.

Life Lesson 7

Live Your Life

L ife is excellent and a true blessing from God. That's why you have to live it to the fullest. Nobody knows when their life will end but it's the faith you have in God that keeps you alive every day. So knowing all of this should surely make you realise that other people's opinions about you hold no weight and your opinion is the most important one. This is why you should always follow your standards. Don't hold yourself to other people's standards; having that mindset will stop you from growing. Create your version of everything and keep yourself motivated by that. You need to do what makes you happy but be cautious because whatever pleases you might be helpful right now but it can still hinder you in the long term. Always think before you do something. Head into everything with a calculated mind, so you know the odds of you doing a good or a great job.

While you live your life, it's important to try different things until you find your passion. When you have found your passion, then my advice is you should follow it. But before you do that, you have to consider many things. Will this sustain you for the rest of your life? Will your future self be proud of the route you went down? I guess you can answer those questions for yourself. I believe in following your passion more than anyone else but please be careful. Re-think that passion you have and look deeper for the one that can help you for the rest of your life. Doing something for the next three years is fantastic; however, sustaining it for the next twenty years is better. Long term thinking cancels short term excitement. When you have found your passion and you've given it enough thought, an easy way to make it sustainable for the rest of your life is to make whatever you're doing revolve around people because nothing multiplies more than human beings. I can't really think of many businesses that don't have people involved so if your company doesn't revolve around people, then find a way to make them essential. Putting yourself in a position that benefits people will make you win for the rest of your life.

This doesn't only apply to people who own businesses or seek to own one in the future. It applies to everyone because no matter where you find yourself in life, you'll be in front of people. How you make people rely on you will be one of the most important things that'll help you excel. You'll be feeding on human needs but every big business in the world feeds on human needs; so you should do the same thing too. Most people think using human beings is a bad thing. On the contrary, I think it's good as long as you're not harming anyone, you can use anyone to your advantage even if they don't like you. This is because most people claim they don't like others, but they're still so invested in what they do. All you need to do is make sure whatever you're doing is good and that's how you'll pull them in because no one completely forgets their experience with others. Even when they do, they'll end up thinking about it again because that's how the human mind works. When they think about you, they'll most likely check what you're doing so they can criticise it. While they're trying to criticise it, there's a good possibility they'll support you by looking at what you're doing. That's why you shouldn't be surprised when your 'haters' become your supporters/customers. It happens because humans lack self-control but you can feed off of it in a positive way by looking at it differently.

An example of a business using humans in a positive way is Microsoft. I am sure Bill Gates wasn't thinking about this when he created it but he literally serves as a core for human beings. This is because we use Microsoft everyday without realising it, some people might even be addicted to it too. And because of that, it's only going to benefit Microsoft down the line. So this is why you should think of something that humans can't live without and make something good because it will help you for the rest of your life. A couple suggestions are clothing, music, art, books and food. I am sure there are a couple more you can think about too.

I am also certain this is not the first time a random stranger is telling you to find your passion. Yes, you've tried before and it's honestly easier said than done. But with the right people around you, you can make anything work. Our relationships – whether familial or romantic – contribute immensely to the overall outcome of our lives. So cherish those who are there for you when you are still trying to figure life out because it is those ones that really love you for who you are and not what you are or about to become. You have to be mindful of the people that are around in the good times and in bad times. Suppose someone that didn't support you when you were at the bottom of your ladder comes back into your life. I would personally cut them off immediately as they return. Not everybody has to be your friend so be mindful of those you call your 'friend.' Life is full of ups and downs and they might change on you the moment something goes wrong. When you live your life and move up the ladder, try your best not to care about who supports you. Everyone does whatever suits their agenda. Most people around you don't have your best interest at heart, so be mindful of those you call your friends. You must be careful enough to only surround yourself with genuine support if you want to go far in life.

If you don't have a passion, then don't be disheartened. There's nothing wrong with that, just try to better yourself every day in the path you choose. We all have one life to live, so make sure you live it like it's your last movie. If you have found your passion, please don't follow it for financial gain. There should be more to it than that, never do it for cash only because you will be running around in circles for the rest of your life. We don't own any of our money when you think about it. We are just basically lending it for a certain period until we spend it, and then it will end up in someone else's hands. That's why being in it only for money will lead you astray because money is always on the move.

What Is Next?

Writing my first book has indeed been a fantastic experience. I told some of my friends on the 23rd of November 2020 that I would write my first book. I didn't start writing until the 1st of January 2021. I was going through a lot during 2020 which made it hard for me to concentrate. I am happy I completed this book, proud of my work. It hasn't been easy, and it is easily the hardest thing I've done in my life so far, but it made me better in so many ways. I now know that putting my ideas in this book is the best thing I ever did. I hope this book helped you learn something about life and get to know me a bit better.

Suppose the book helped you, then don't hesitate to message me (see the book's end for my contact details). If it didn't help you, then please message me too. I need all the feedback I can get because I love doing this, and I plan to release more books after university. After you finish reading the book, please leave me some feedback and give it an honest rating on Amazon. I will be reading all of it and using it to make my future books better. Share it to your family and friends because it might be helpful to them too. Right now, my main focus is finishing university and also growing my book business. I am sure you are wondering why I didn't drop out of university after everything I've put myself through. The main reasons why I didn't are because I want to prove something to myself, and I also see some sort of importance in having a degree. I also didn't enjoy sports science. I tried changing several times but they told me I would have to wait until the end of the year. If I had gotten good grades on my first attempt, then I would've been able to change. I don't regret doing what I did during my first two years of university because it taught me valuable lessons that brought me to where I am today. Even after everything I experienced, it made my life better in every aspect, so I'm forever grateful for what happened to me.

My life right now is far from perfect; there's still so much painful stuff I don't talk about. But I try to see the positives in every negative situation. I still have problems and situations to deal with, but I know no one can be perfect. I just try my best to do better than I did the day before. I also noticed that problems actually never go away. As you go up the ladder in your life, you just encounter better problems. I like to call them: 'problems you wouldn't mind having.' Some are still worse but you can pick your battles by remembering not to stress about the things you can't control. Realising this helped me be at peace with life and everything that comes with it.

I hope you learned something valuable from this book. I know you are destined for greatness, so use some parts of my life and lessons to help you during your marathon. Always run your own marathon and not someone else's.

Thank you for purchasing my first book and taking time out of your life to hear my story so far. I wish you the very best in the future, and may God continue to bless you and your family.

Ursino Obamudi 2021

Acknowledgements

I would not have written this book without Femi Opedo, Jordan Adelekan, Ayomide Adeyanju, Kieran Murray, Evans Okungbowa Fuerte, Adam Sylla, Daniel Yaroson, Dilan Kang, Joseph Nganje, Aj Oluwasina, Victoria Amunikoro ,Tobi Hassan, Natalie Sem, Leah Balogun, Layla J Pinnock, Elizabeth Adekoya, Sean Karuru, Emmanuel Osaro, Asher Hines, Leah Ocean, Michelle Egbe, Maggie Kileke, Junior Hombo, Reuben Chumpuka, Ademola Osiniwo, Israel Daniel, Brian Enninful, Ohenmaa Welbeck and Kemi Awoleke.

I want to thank everyone that has supported me one way or another, through sinobills or booksbybills.

I also want to thank my parents and siblings because, without them, this would not be possible.

I love all of you.

Ursino Obamudi

Want to Speak To Ursino Obamudi?

Ursino Obamudi speaks to many people about life. He talks to them according to their requirements and makes sure to see things from their point of view too. His goal is to do whatever he can do to help others in their personal and practical life. He aims to deliver his messages effectively.

For more information on how to speak to Ursino Obamudi, you can contact him on:

Instagram: @sinobills

Twitter: @sinobills

Snapchat: @sinobills

TikTok: @booksbybills

Email: uobamudi@icloud.com

Website: www.booksbybills.co.uk

Printed in Great Britain
by Amazon